Minimalism

Living in a Small and Clutter-Free Environment

The Science of Living

Fhilcar Faunillan

Mendon Cottage Books

JD-Biz Publishing

Disclaimer

The information is this book is provided for informational purposes only. It is not intended to be used and medical advice or a substitute for proper medical treatment by a qualified health care provider. The information is believed to be accurate as presented based on research by the author.

The contents have not been evaluated by the U.S. Food and Drug Administration or any other Government or Health Organization and the contents in this book are not to be used to treat cure or prevent disease.

The author or publisher is not responsible for the use or safety of any diet, procedure, or treatment mentioned in this book. The author or publisher is not responsible for errors or omissions that may exist.

Warning

The Book is for informational purposes only and before taking on any diet, treatment, or medical procedure, it is recommended to consult with your primary health care provider.

Our books are available at
1. Amazon.com
2. Barnes and Noble
3. Itunes
4. Kobo
5. Smashwords
6. Google Play Books

Table of Contents

Introduction

Minimalism is a way of living that cuts the gluttony surrounding our world. It is the exact opposite of what we see in ads, what we hear on the radio, or what commercials air on TV. It contrasts what our society has etched on our minds regarding the claimed importance of accumulating stuff. It tells us to dismiss ourselves from consumerism, instead of priding ourselves for all our material possessions, the clutters in our environment, the skyrocketing debts, and an abundance of infinite distractions.

People are joining the craze of the material world and we are left with a meaningless one. People are crazy over lots of stuff, with closets full of clothes, racks full of shoes, garages stacked with useless gears, basements cluttered with boxes of what seems like hoarding of old items. They are living the typical life: working hard to make good money, spend a great chunk on it to pay for mortgage, buy fancy clothes, and keep up with friends who have luxury cars, or get a hand of cool technology which are seen as bragging rights.

It is hard to see and realize that we do not need any of these, and that life is more meaningful when there are no people to impress, that we do not have to spend so much on stuff we don't need just to make us happy, and that a rise in pay wouldn't necessarily mean a rise in cost of living. It takes a turning point to make people aware that they are losing themselves over their material possessions. And this point could be achieved by the continuous effort of dissenters who encourage a simpler, less materialist life.

Living a minimalist lifestyle means throwing out what you do not need and focus only on those that you need. We only need little to survive while still living happily. We only need the small things to keep content in our hearts. The stuff that surround us are only depictions of materialism, and the society telling us that we have to consume more of it is just a way of luring us into consumerism. These things do not matter and do not account for our own happiness.

Chapter 1: Own Less, Live Best

Minimalism as a way of life allows people to question the things they value most in their lives. It allows the uncluttering of the mind, the surroundings, and of life as whole, to make room for what really matters in life such as health, social relationships, personal growth, and contribution to other people.

As we see it, more people are living the materialist lifestyle because they grew up to the sight of it. The culture and the get-all-you-want mentality have prevailed and shaped the minds and behaviors of people over time. This is exactly the reason why we see a continuous trend of overconsumption being passed from one generation to the next. There are many countries which value this kind of lifestyle, which makes it hard to revolt for a minimalist lifestyle.

Living a minimalist lifestyle does not really pertain to anti-consumption, but it refers more to anti-overconsumption. Not all things that we have are compulsory possessions, nor are they of significance to our own survival. By jettisoning and ditching the excess stuff in your life and the things that do not add value to it, you are making the first few steps towards a more rewarding life. Later, you will realize that these possessions were not merely physical manifestations of a cluttered environment, but it is a representation of a deeper problem, which is an internal clutter in the mind and soul.

If you are living the materialist lifestyle, you should be asking yourself whether this or that possession adds value to your life. It may turn out that more than 50 percent of what you own does not add value at all, and that you should start getting rid of all these things.

Most of us take bad turns and search for happiness in the wrong places. Our society has provided us with a map to happiness and we are told to follow it. We believe it. However, people who have gone through this maze map to happiness will tell you they did not find genuine happiness at all. There are actually many paths to happiness and finding the right one takes great effort. What society has been telling us do not make any sense at all because happiness is just around the corner, waiting for it to be realized. To live a more meaningful life, you should own only those that serve you purpose or bring you genuine happiness.

Intentionality for Minimalist Lifestyle

People need to experience losing themselves in the hype of materialism because is when they look deep in their hearts and thought about life of meaninglessness. By this time, people look for an outlet or relief of living life from paycheck to paycheck. It is when they become tired of splurging their money, knowing that other people needed it more, or when they finally become weary of the stresses they get with mortgage repayments, monthly bills, and other high-maintenance stuff.

Intentionally deciding to live a minimalist life and have fewer possessions is often motivated by an endless cycle of discontentment. This motivation to live meaningfully opens the doors for freedom, productivity, satisfaction, improved social relationships, and a whole lot more.

Deciding to be a minimalist could stem from different aspects in life. This could be found in the beliefs and passions that a person holds. Each one of us has different beliefs of what makes us happy. By defining these, we can pursue our passion and find intentionality from it. If your happiness is spending more time with family, then you should find ways be with family by living the minimalist way.

Intentionally living a minimalist life could also come from our care for finances. When we own less, we do not only get more money, but we get more opportunity to invest our money. When we are successfully attracted to a minimalist lifestyle and discharge ourselves from consumerism, we can make use of our money for more valuable things, more than just the clearance rack at the department store.

There is no reason we can't make help available to others. And because of this, more significant decisions are made.

Some people also choose to live the minimalist lifestyle because of concern for health. We experience stress, anxiety, and other problems that may affect some systems of our body because we are too engrossed with the thought of money. We sweat the money problems, making life less enjoyable.

When we live minimally, we also become very conscious with what we put in our bodies. By taking the time to cook our own food and make healthy food choices, we are doing a favor for our own health. Instead of spending your money by eating at a fast food restaurant, or buying any other processed food from the supermarket, you should start growing your own fruits and vegetables, and that is surely organic.

Other turning point to live a simple life includes our concern for spirituality. With a minimalist lifestyle, we can slow ourselves down and take time to look at ourselves and question what has become of us. We will realize that our life has been hijacked to think of the advertisements that drive us to consume. The principles of minimalism encourage us to find solitary time and meditation. These new guiding principles lead us to a better path in life.

We also find the intention to live simply when we see that we need to be more connected with other people around us. When we are not busy hoarding stuff, we are giving more time for other people in our lives. We become deeply connected with our neighbors and the community. We welcome more people to our homes and make their arrival easier. When we start to shift from spending our time on shopping and cluttering, we can spend more time with the people who make our life a lot more enjoyable, and our capacity to build new relationships only grows.

Moreover, when we realize we are only working for the money, we can turn to the minimalist life. And when we begin to live with only little stuff, our view about money begins to change and it only becomes less important. Once our basic needs are met, we can make use of money to show generosity to others who need it. As our view of money shifts, our motivation to do our jobs also shifts. Working is no longer about the salary we get, but it focuses more on the value of contribution we provide.

Choosing to live a minimalist lifestyle opens our doors for contentment, generosity, and deeper meaning in life. It allows us to redefine happiness. Happiness is no longer a retail therapy or the clearance sale of a local store. Instead, it is a decision laid in front of us all along. Minimalism is adapted as a way of life because of discontent. However, the greatest gift brought about from this discontentment is finding intentionality to live a more meaningful life.

Chapter 2: Benefits of Minimalism

Having a minimalist lifestyle does not mean living cheap, boring, or less enjoyable. The minimalist life involves reduction of what is in excess. There is obviously a bunch of benefits from this such as less areas to clean, more organized home, more opportunities to invest in, and greater satisfaction in life. When we get rid of excess stuff, what we fail to realize is that we are removing more than just stuff. These are some of the benefits of having a minimalist lifestyle:

1. Make room for greater things

When we clear our drawers, closets, basements, and other areas where we would normally junk our stuff, we are creating more space. Making room for greater things does not only pertain to physical items. It also means freeing ourselves with distractions in life. When we have organized and clean surroundings, we achieve a peace of mind. We give more space for meaning instead of stuff.

2. Gain more freedom

Being so absorbed with material possessions hinder us to happiness. This gluttony serves as an anchor that ties us to the mentality of wanting more stuff. We believe that having more translates to being more valued, thus we are always scared of losing what we have. But when we let go of all these things, we experience freedom from greed, heavy debts, money problems, stresses from overwork, and obsession with materials.

3. More time for hobbies

When you stop keeping up with the latest trends in fashion or the latest in technology, you can spend more time doing what you love, and explore other things that you may be interested in. Most people reason that they don't have the luxury of time to do what they want. But when we look deeper, how many people actually stop and take time to see what they have been busy doing all along? You say you want to do gardening with kids, practice yoga on weekends, read good books or go travel. But you don't realize that you are stuck up at Sears buying more stuff.

4. Happiness independent of material possessions

The stuff we buy for ourselves and the abundance of stuff in stores are distractions from living a simpler life. Buying more stuff is like filling a void and we are using money to buy what we think could give us happiness. However, our money could only afford comfort. The media continues to bombard us with ads that promise us happiness with material possessions. It is not so surprising why we struggle every day of our lives trying to resist the impulse and temptations. We have been hardwired to consume more, and so we always need to be reminded that this path does not bring us happiness. We may enjoy stuff, but we should recognize that we don't need all of it.

5. An uncluttered mind

Once we have attached ourselves to material possessions, we are building up stress within ourselves and then we tend to be afraid of losing all these stuff. We let our possessions define who we are. However, when we make our life simple by pulling off the strings from all these stuff, we can have a more peaceful mind. The less we worry, the more peace we can have.

6. Find happiness in the smallest things

Once you unclutter your life, you will find more happiness as you settle only for what matters most. You can clearly distinguish the false promises from all the clutters because it is like a broken shield that stands out from the true essence in life. There is more happiness when you have prioritized your needs, and there is joy when you start slowing down.

7. Greater confidence

When you have already let go of all the worldly possessions, there is only you. You become stronger and you are not afraid of anything because there is nothing to lose. You are more confident that you will be able to rely on yourself no matter what happens, and be more assured that you will find happiness in the right places.

Chapter 3: Getting Your Life Back

You have to set your mind to get your life back. It takes mental fortitude to commit to owning less. You have to make a decision for every item that you have; and that could be mentally draining especially if you own a lot. If it took you so much time collecting all your possessions, it will certainly take much more time to sort these out.

Preparing to sort your things doesn't have to take long. You can start the sorting process by preparing boxes for every room and when you come across things you think you don't need, throw them in the box. You really have to prepare getting the right mindset because whether we believe it or not, we are attached to most of our things. However, these things have a catch. The big house you are afraid of letting go and everything else that comes with it take so much time to clean and organize, and worse, it takes so much money for maintenance. Look at all your possessions and think about how long you have to work to own it. Every piece of it could have gained you time or money if you sell and give it up.

The right time to do it is now. Think about the different areas in your life where you get so frustrated. Think about when you have to make so many decisions, in choosing your clothes or in looking for items at a disorganized room. Point out those areas and deal with them. Start a garage sale or sell them on eBay.

Uncluttering your life could last longer so you have to start small. You can't do it in a day. The processes are daunting and if you are anxious about these changes, start with those things that are easy to get rid of. Ditch those that are obviously unused for several years, the mugs don't use, the magazines you don't plan on reading, or those ugly stuff you received as gifts. Furniture and other large household items which take so much space should be discarded. It wouldn't be very difficult to part with your items when you see you have passed them to people who needed it more. Unlike throwing them directly to the garbage, you may only feel like you have wasted so much.

Once you have sold your stuff and stopped buying new ones, have the money serve a different purpose. Once you stopped from frittering your money on junk, you can put it on more essentials for the house, retirement, and meaningful experiences.

Assess how you feel about uncluttering your life. The next time you thought about buying something, always remember to make only smart purchases. Shop when it is needed, not because you are bored or want to be entertained. Make an inventory of the things you have so you are less likely to buy another version of it. Count the things you have and it will discourage you from getting something new. And when you are looking to buy an item, choose those that serve several purposes.

One of the bigger changes that you can undertake is moving from a big home to a smaller one. Big homes are not for everyone, and so if you are struggling to pay the mortgage, downsizing your home may help you accomplish more. You will be more inclined to get lesser stuff, lesser space to clean, and smaller bills.

Becoming a Minimalist

Starting the process of changing your lifestyle could be done in a few, but effortful steps. You can slowly become a minimalist. As previously mentioned, you can find intentionality from different the aspects in your life. In the previous chapter, you have also learned the things you need to know when getting your life back. But how do you actually start the process? If you are a beginner minimalist or off to your journey to a simpler life, take a look at these steps.

1. Set your mind

The mind controls your behavior and it is important to set it according to the minimalist principles to successfully proceed in uncluttering your life. You have to have the discipline, control, and focus in order to keep in line with your mission to live a minimalist life. Once you are mentally ready, you can proceed and move forward.

2. Jot down your reasons

List all the reasons why you want to live a simpler life. Are you tired of monthly bills that take a chunk of your income? Are you mad that you never get the time to spend with significant others? Are you stressed about money problems? Are you sick of being a corporate slave to your bosses? Are you in heavy load from debts? Write them on paper. Those will be your reasons why and it will serve as great leverage when you feel that it is hard to keep going on in life with all those problems.

3. Ditch the duplicates

Look around your home, take the duplicates and place them in a box. If you have 5 mugs, maybe it's time that you give away the other three. If you have a rack of unused shoes, maybe it's time you give them to the homeless. You only need a few pair of shoes to get to where you're going. Having same copies of books? Donate the rest of the copies. You don't need to store duplicates. You only need one of everything.

4. Make a clutter-free zone

If you have an area at home which you could use as kitchen table, nightstands, a drawer, then do it. Use that zone and make it an inspiration to live minimally. If you feel happy about the environment, slowly expand the zone and every day. Having a clutter-free countertop may slowly turn into a clutter-free room and this may entirely lead to becoming the minimalist home you have been dreaming of.

5. Learn from your travels

Travelling allows you to practice your minimalist lifestyle, unless you are the leisure traveler type. The next time you go out of town, always renew your love for minimalism by packing half the time. If you are travelling for 10 days, pack clothes enough for 5 days. You can simply wash your clothes at your destination and wear the same clothes twice. You will realize the comfort you get when carrying light baggage, same feeling you get when you only have few things.

6. Cook your own meal

Calculate the total money you have spent eating at a restaurant and compare it with the amount you spend when cooking your own food. You will realize that you could have saved big amounts from that. Moreover, you could also save more when you also grow your own food. Not only that, you are sure you are eating organic foods, free of other preservatives. You are contributing to both your pocket and your diet.

7. Save for an emergency fund

Your emergency funds will save you when it rains hard. Making money for emergencies reduces the anxiety and stress you get when problems occur. Try building funds for emergency purposes and feel a lot more confident about your finances.

Even if it will take you years to achieve the minimalist life, the benefits come immediately. Try out different ways of living minimally. The journey towards it can be very flexible, and as a beginner, you may also be more curious and daring.

Other Ways to Maximize Life

1. Stop organizing

You don't have to organize your things and do it over again. It takes so much effort to keep on organizing. So if you haven't touched those items for months, then give it away. Don't store it in your home.

2. Stop looking for bargains

Only buy what you need. Doesn't mean because it's on clearance sale you should take it. The next time you visit the local store, list down what you need and focus only on buying those items instead of detouring through the sales booth.

3. Spend your time wisely

The average person spends 8 hours every week cleaning and organizing stuff. The time spent organizing could have been spent as a leisure time. By uncluttering your home, you will spend lesser time cleaning, and so purging would appear as relaxation time in the future.

4. Stop keeping up with fashion

Give your wardrobe a break and wear simpler clothes. You don't have to buy lots of clothes to keep yourself in fashion. As long as you can confidently carry yourself, you don't have to dress yourself with the most fashionable clothes.

5. Don't add new knick-knacks

If you are trying to unclutter your home, it follows that you must not buy new unnecessary things. There is no sense trying to get rid of unused items when you are adding up new ones.

6. Keep the counters clean

When your juicer or any other items don't fit your cabinets, start asking yourself if you still need that item or if you could warrant looking at that every day.

7. Don't stop uncluttering

Uncluttering your environment is a process. You can't unclutter once and then go back to your old lifestyle. It is a long process that becomes a habit later on, so be vigilant in finding new clutters at home.

8. Travel more

When you go on a backpacker style kind of travel, you will learn many ways of living minimally. Try travelling for weeks while packing your things in a 35-liter backpack. You will realize just how small you need to survive a few weeks outside your own home.

9. Don't be consumed by consumerism

Furnish your house luxuriously by taking out the unnecessary stuff from your home, instead of taking more stuff to ornament your home.

Minimalism in Homes

Minimalism is not for everyone. However, with the world that we live in, we feel that we are called to live such life—to own less, to spend less, and need less.

Where does the road start for having minimalist homes? There are numerous beginners map that will lead you to a minimalist home. None of these will instantly turn your life the way you wanted it to be. But you can get some ideas that will help you in your journey towards having a minimalist home.

You have probably read about our folks who have made huge changes in their life, letting go of almost everything they have, and moving to this all-white room with just their mattress and notepad. You probably want to get to that similar path to minimalism, or maybe you want to achieve it in some other ways, gradually. Take out your list and start on what resounds most to you.

Make a clear goal and timeline. Define your idea of a minimalist home. Is it about having the minimum of items? Is it about clearing your whole home of stuff you haven't used for months? Is it to stop buying on things that you do not need? There are many ways to becoming minimalist and there is no exact or right way of becoming one. If you can't figure out what you don't want for your house, then take the time to determine what you want for your home or what makes you feel relaxed and stress-free. From there, begin stripping away these things that hinder you from getting your ideal uncluttered home.

Once you have set clear goals, steps, and timeline to achieve your desired home, you can start with the process. Along the way, always remind yourself of the reasons why you want to have a minimalist home, and that will leverage or motivate you towards achieving your home goals. In addition, tell yourself of the benefits you could get from having a minimalist home. You can do this by travelling to some places and get to live in homes which match your ideal home size. From there, you can determine whether you are comfortable living in such home, or you need some more upsize or downsize.

Once you are mentally and emotionally ready to get started living in a minimalist home, start uncluttering. This is probably the most painful part for most folks because of the attachment that comes with items. For years, people have identified themselves with what they own. However, you can always start slow by donating everything those that you don't need. It would be a lot less painful when you see your things utilized in charities or other people who needed it more. You could also hide some of your things first and try doing without it for months to give distance between you and your things. Later on, you can give them away. Once you have uncluttered a few things, it would be easier for you to unclutter more items. And by doing so, you are making your path easier to having a minimalist home and lifestyle. Again, living minimally doesn't mean living in a room with a bed and a notepad. You decide on your own what a minimalist home is to you. While in the process of uncluttering your home, also start to train yourself living with less possession. If you used to be a creature for comfort, don't abruptly plunge to having a minimal home all at once. Start by giving yourself comfort days every month until you have slowly eliminated the comforts or luxuries of your old home, then you will eventually realize that it is okay to lose the luxuries and still be happy.

In addition, always be mindful before even swiping your credit card for a purchase. Make it a habit to ask yourself whether you need an item before buying them. Remember that it is very easy to justify purchases, but when you ask yourself, you will see that you don't really need those things and that you bought those out of impulsivity. One way of avoiding buying things out of impulse is to practice reuse. You can save packaging and reuse it later for other stuff. Repair broken things instead of replacing these with new ones. Use available scrap or fabrics and start a DIY project. Spark your creativity and create new things by using old ones. Moreover, you could also invest for high-quality materials so that you don't end up buying new ones when something gets broken.

Along the way, you may find that you have undergone great challenge in pursuing a minimalist home and lifestyle. When you think that it gets tough trying to pursue the minimalist life, always remind yourself of the reasons why you want to live minimally. Think about the reasons why you have intentionally decided to live pursue a minimalist life in the first place. This will spark the motivation you need to keep trying. The quest for simplicity is not simple especially that we grew up living in the standards of the society, and being consumed by consumerism for years. However, there is also no reason why we should give up looking for simplicity in the right places.

Conclusion

The idea of living in a minimalist and clutter-free environment certainly resonates to most people. However, it is a surprisingly difficult process to start with. The current generation grew up being bombarded with what society claims to be a standard of living, which centers largely on consumerism. We have been told to consume more, to wear fashionable clothes, to own designer bags, to live in a big house, own a luxury car, and compete with others in terms of material possessions because having more would mean having high social status.

With the great influence of society on our lives, it is no wonder why it is so hard to let go of our worldly possessions and enjoy being slaves of the society. But why don't we challenge ourselves and strip off all these standards set by the society? Why don't we start defining our own life and live according to what really make us happy? Why don't we start acting now?

It is a challenge for the millenials to start making the change and bring back the old and simpler lifestyle. If the extravagant lifestyles that most people enjoy continue to be passed on to the next generation, we will be left with a world defined by consumerism. We will be left with a world with no meaning. We can't let that happen.

Author Bio

Fhilcar Faunillan

Born in the central part of the Philippines, Fhilcar Faunillan developed her interest in a lot of things – pets, gardening, urban and rural living, prepping, culinary and travel. There she finished her business and law degree and has spent some years teaching in college while doing some business of sorts.

Her love for writing and sharing her experiences, doing charitable works and exploring new ideas as well as extending help to children whose basic education needs to be assisted never ceased as she is in the process of putting up her own learning center.

Fhilcar's horizon seems limitless as she embraces the changes around her but critically thinks of their practical relevance.

Check out some of the other JD-Biz Publishing books

Gardening Series on Amazon

Health Learning Series

GRANDMA'S NATURAL REMEDIES AND ANCIENT HERBAL BEAUTY RECIPES — *Volume 1*
HEALTH LEARNING SERIES
DULEEP J SINGH AND J DAVIDSON

GRANDMA'S NATURAL REMEDIES AND ANCIENT HERBAL BEAUTY RECIPES — *Volume 2*
HEALTH LEARNING SERIES
DULEEP J SINGH AND J DAVIDSON

GRANDMA'S NATURAL REMEDIES AND ANCIENT RECIPES
GRANDMA'S CURE FOR OBESITY
GRANDMA'S CURE FOR THE COMMON COLD
Volume 3
HEALTH LEARNING SERIES
DULEEP J SINGH AND J DAVIDSON

GRANDMA'S NATURAL REMEDIES AND ANCIENT HERBAL RECIPES
Volume 4
HEALTH LEARNING SERIES
DULEEP J SINGH AND J DAVIDSON

GRANDMA'S HERBAL LORE ANCIENT HERBAL RECIPES AND REMEDIES
Volume 5
HEALTH LEARNING SERIES
DULEEP J SINGH AND J DAVIDSON

GRANDMA'S ANCIENT BEAUTY REMEDIES FROM HER KITCHEN
Volume 6
HEALTH LEARNING SERIES
DULEEP J SINGH AND J DAVIDSON

GRANDMA'S EASY TO USE TIPS IN THE KITCHEN AND OUTDOORS
Volume 7

HEALTH LEARNING SERIES
DULEEP J SINGH AND J DAVIDSON

GRANDMA'S HOUSEHOLD HINTS AND RECIPES USING TIME TESTED ECONOMICAL TIPS IN YOUR HOME
75 Tips
Remove Stains
Peel Tomatoes — Perfect Pies
HEALTH LEARNING SERIES
DULEEP J SINGH AND J DAVIDSON

GRANDMA'S NATURAL REMEDIES AND ANCIENT RECIPES
ALL 5 BOOKS IN 1

HEALTH LEARNING SERIES
DULEEP J SINGH AND J DAVIDSON

Country Life Books

Health Learning Series

Amazing Animal Book Series

Learn To Draw Series

How to Build and Plan Books

Entrepreneur Book Series

Our books are available at

1. Amazon.com

2. Barnes and Noble

3. Itunes

4. Kobo

5. Smashwords

6. Google Play Books

Publisher

JD-Biz Corp

P O Box 374

Mendon, Utah 84325

http://www.jd-biz.com/

www.ingramcontent.com/pod-product-compliance
Lightning Source LLC
Chambersburg PA
CBHW070517290526
45790CB00003B/1249